KAREL HUSA

FRAMMENTI

for Solo Organ

AMP-8031
First Printing: May 1992

ASSOCIATED MUSIC PUBLISHERS, Inc.

Distributed by
Hal Leonard Publishing Corporation
7777 West Bluemound Road   P.O. Box 13819   Milwaukee, Wisconsin 53213

Frammenti (fragments) was extracted from Husa's *Concerto for Organ and Orchestra* (1987) at the suggestion of Karel Paukert, who was the soloist in the premiere of the *Concerto* at the Cleveland Museum of Art on October 28, 1987 with the composer conducting the Cleveland Institute of Music Orchestra. Mr. Paukert premiered *Frammenti* on November 6, 1987 at Northwestern University in Evanston, Illinois.

The *Concerto* was commissioned as part of the Michelson-Morley Centennial Celebration, which commemorates the historic Michelson-Morley experiment that marked the birth of modern physics and paved the way for Einstein's theory of relativity. Husa was aware of the special nature of this celebration and took light as his theme: specifically, sunlight in its many moods. In fact, he originally thought of titling his work *Sunlights*—a title, Mr. Husa points out, that would work better in French: *Les lumières de soleil.* The inspiration for the *Concerto,* according to Husa, is the "sunlight constantly surrounding us, creating powerful images, colors, and shades in the sky and on the earth." The image of light refracted through glass, through a church or temple window, was also a stimulus to the composer.

—REBECCA FISCHER

duration: ca. 6 minutes

FRAMMENTI
I

Karel Husa

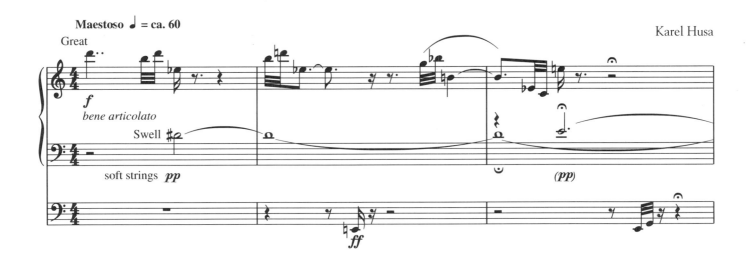

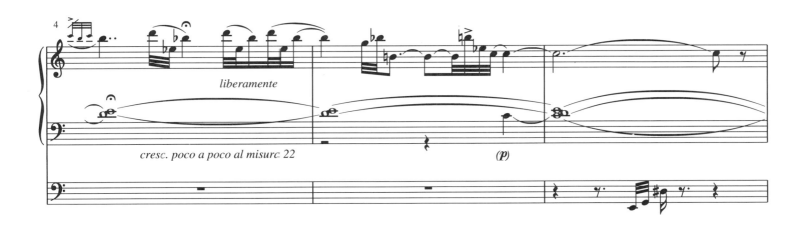

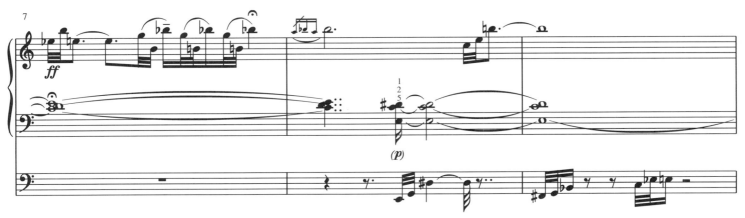

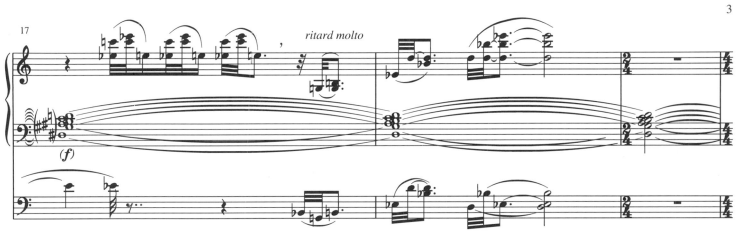

II

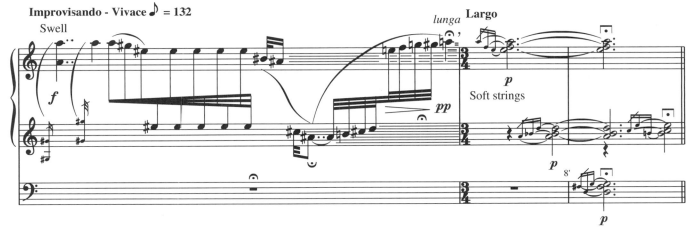

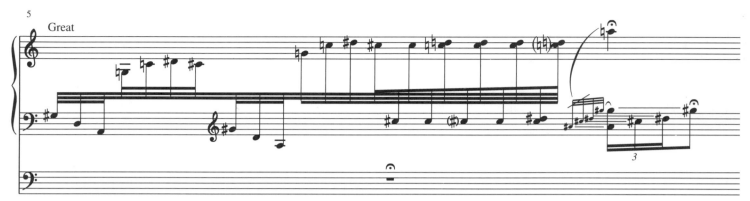

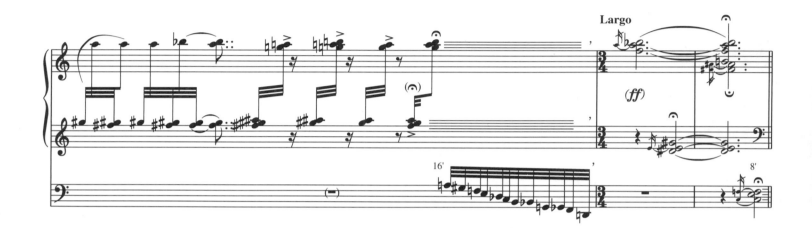

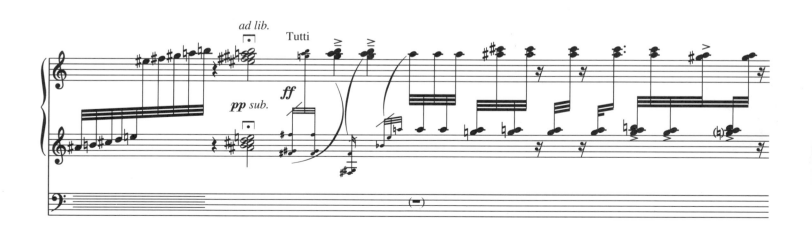

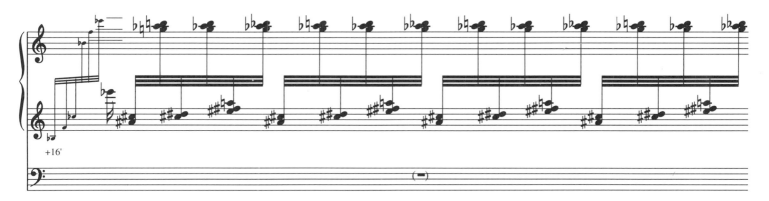

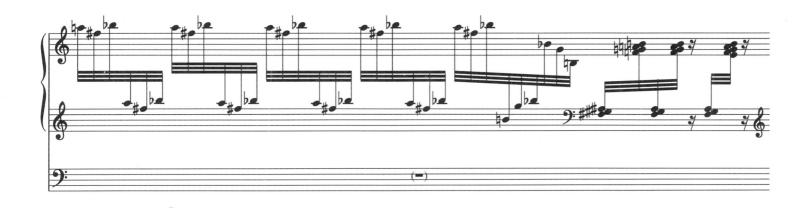

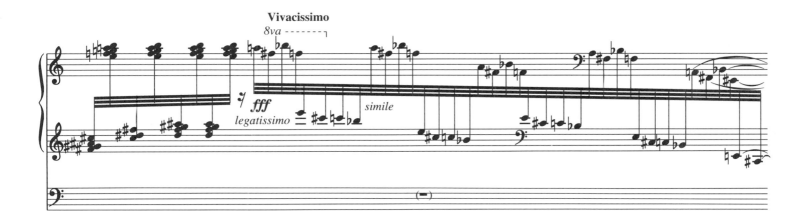

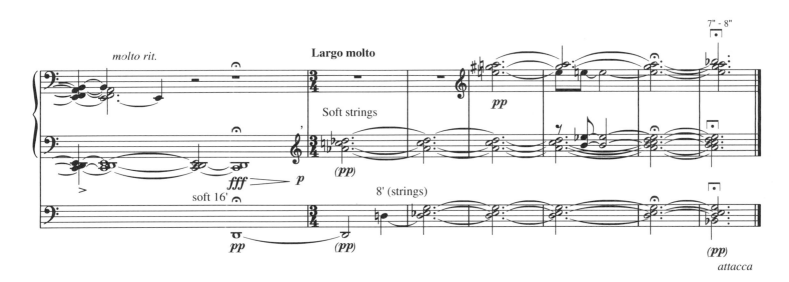

III

accelerando poco a poco